Unofficial

Trapped in TikTok 4

Halloween

ViralReadz

CONTENTS

1

The Halloween of Nightmares

I couldn't believe what was happening. All of my friends were zombies, and worse, they were fast approaching me. *Will they give me a hug? Will they try to eat me?* I had no idea. I stepped backward more and more, until I could feel my back hit something hard. I had nowhere to escape, and these zombies, though very slow, were getting worryingly closer to me. I checked myself for a weapon, but I had nothing to protect myself.

I would have hoped that, since I was dressed like a zombie, these zombies might mistake me for one of their own. But my awesome costume was no use; they could tell I was actually a human merely dressed as a zombie. The zombies' arms reached out as they all crowded around me, almost engulfing me. This was the end for me and my wacky adventures...

2

The Weird Award Ceremony

"Stacey!!"

Whenever my mom shouted my name, it was never good. I was still in bed, and it was a Saturday too, so I should have been allowed to sleep a bit longer.

"I'm sleeping!" I replied. There was a loud pounding on my bedroom door. I really didn't want to get out of bed; it was so cold outside, and I was as snug as a bug in a rug.

"If you're sleeping, then how come you just replied? A letter came for you, and it looks important!" said Mom. A letter? Who would send me a letter? It wasn't my birthday, and I had no pen pals.

"OK, I'm coming! Just chill!" I grumbled. I launched myself out of my bed and threw on some clothes before darting down the stairs. Mom was waiting by the kitchen table with this mysterious letter in the middle like a decoration.

"So? Open it, sweetie!" urged Mom. I rolled my eyes and reached out my arm over to grab the letter. I studied it closely for a clue but all it said was my name, no address or special symbols, it's as though it was delivered by hand. I flaunt the letter at mom jokingly before opening it up.

You have been invited to a special award ceremony tonight, with a special award in your name as thanks for saving the world!

"Saving the world? When was that?" inquired my curious mom. I rolled my eyes again.

"I have done it, like, three times now I think... Aren't you suppose to say congratulations?" I giggled. Mom nodded.

"Oh, yeaH, sorry. Congratulations! Is that all it says?" replied Mom. I shook my head;there was something else.

The ceremony is located in the special events hall located downtown. Dress code: Halloween. It begins at 7pm! We look forward to your attendance!

"Halloween? That's today! Oh wow! I have no idea what to wear! I can't believe I am winning an award!" I shouted. Mom stood up and walked over towards me, giving me a warm hug.

"Oh sweetie, this is really amazing! I am so proud!" Mom whispered into my ear. I felt proud of myself—it's not that often I win an award. Before I could say anything else, my phone began beeping like crazy. I pulled it from my pocket to take a look, and it was the gang. They were all messaging about getting invited to the award ceremony too. As I scrolled through the messages, I even saw that some of the my friends were already heading to the event on a private plane. A reunion and an award, this couldn't get any better! I didn't have time to message back. I needed to think of what to wear!

"Hmm, what should I dress as for Halloween, Mom?" I asked. She looked around the room for inspiration.

"Well, last year you went as me! So maybe this year go as your dad!"

"I can't do that; I have an award ceremony to go to!" I replied.

"Hmm, well, why not dress as something that reflects your personality.

Let's see, you sit on your phone all day watching TikTok, and you make silly sounds… I know! A zombie!" *Wow*.

"Mom! Actually, though, I've never been a zombie… good idea! Can you drop me off at the award ceremony? Pretty please?" I begged. Mom rolled *her* eyes at *me* for once.

"Sweetie, if you can save the world, you can find your own way there. Besides, your father and I have to take your little brother trick or treating, sorry!" Typical. I knew Mom loved trick or treating as much as my brother. She *loved* candy.

"Fine!" I groaned. Part of me was annoyed, but then again, she was finally not treating me like a little kid.

If I wanted to get there, I could always take my bike, although I was a little rusty on it. I looked at my phone to see it was almost 11 a.m. I didn't have much time to prepare, so I needed to act fast.

It was close to 6 by the time I was ready with my costume. What?! I had to improvise. Most of the costume stores were out of stock. Luckily, I found an ugly dress that belonged to my mom, and I used some of my dad's shoe polish to complete my authentic zombie look. I looked pretty scary. I entered the garage and pulled out my old bike from a thousand years ago. I pushed it out of the garage, jumped on and cycled as fast as I could, hoping I wouldn't arrive late.

I made it with only a few minutes to spare. I threw my bike on the ground like a toddler having a tantrum and rushed through the big front doors. As soon as I entered, I was met with a group of random strangers, all dressed in costumes too.

“Are you guys here for the award ceremony? I really hope you are!” I said.

“Stacey?” a clown replied. What the…

“Who are you?” I demanded. I was ready to scream—the clown costume was terrifying.

“It’s me! Xander! We’re all here!” Phew! I was so terrified for a moment. I didn’t know who to hug first, I was so happy. The entire gang was back and looking so ghoulish too. We all got into a circle and did a much-needed group hug.

Suddenly, everything around us shook and large steel plates surrounded us.

I screamed.

"I have no idea what's happening!" replied Frankenstein.

"I don't know either!" shouted a mermaid.

"Oh no! It must be a trap!" yelled a witch.

All my friends were dressed so well in their Halloween costumes that I couldn't really tell who was who, but none of that mattered.

Welcome back! It has been a long time since you were all together! There is no award ceremony, and this is no Halloween trick. If you want to escape, you need to perform a set of challenges... TikTok style!

That voice? It sounded familiar.

"What is going on? Who is this?" I shouted. There was no response.

"Hey, there's a camera there in the corner!" said Xander as he pointed upward. Somebody was watching us...

"What do we do?" I replied. Before we could figure out a plan, the room shook again and a hole opened above us. A huge steel cylinder slowly pierced through, and as it made its way to the ground, we realized it was an elevator.

"I guess we all need to go in? There's nowhere else to go..." said someone dressed as a ghost.

"Ashley?" I recognised her voice, even if she was dressed as a something super spooky. The ghost nodded; it was her!

Everyone shuffled into the mysterious elevator, unsure where it was going to take us.

3

Clowning Around

As the elevator descended, we all stood in silence. Eventually, after what felt like forever, the elevator stopped. We all glanced at each other for some kind of reassurance. The elevator doors opened and a thick smoke poured inside. We all slowly shuffled out of the elevator and into the unknown.

As we each took a step into the unfamiliar room, we all noticed something different.

“Why are there weird laughing sounds?”

“What are those freaky toys?”

“What’s with the clown dolls?”

We were all trying to figure out so much and yet struggled to come to a conclusion. Moments after we all left the elevator, its doors closed and it descended into the floor, disappearing completely.

To escape this room, one of you must perform a funny challenge. Just make sure your humor doesn’t stink. Time is ticking, TikTokers...

A funny challenge? Who should do that? I gazed around the room and then noticed there was only one of us who fit the description—Xander.

“Xander, you’re already dressed as a clown. Can you act like one?” I asked. Everyone went silent.

“Just because I am dressed as a clown, and we are in a room full of clowns, doesn’t mean that I can be a clown!” Xander said.

“Wait. I’ve done this before! There are clues around to figure out what to do... Part of the challenge is finding these clues,” explained Ashley.

“What do you mean?” I asked. I had never heard of an escape room, but I wanted to escape as badly as everyone else. Ashley ignored my response and walked around the room. She darted towards something in particular that really caught her attention.

"Here—there are three clown dolls in a row on a shelf, but the middle one is sad while the other two are happy!"

Xander intervened at this point. He moved closer to the middle clown doll and pulled it off of the shelf. Suddenly, the middle doll began farting loudly.

"What in the...!" screeched Xander. The middle doll farted so loud that everyone struggled to hear anything else.

"You must have started the challenge!" yelped Ashley. "Your challenge must be to use it some way? The voice said to make sure your humor doesn't stink..."

Xander seemed puzzled. I thought so, anyway. It was hard to tell with the clown makeup. Xander held the farting doll for a moment before placing it back on the shelf, probably hoping it might stop it. It continued to fart loudly, so Xander grabbed it and looked around in desperation for something else.

"I don't know what to do!"

"You're a comedian, use your skills here! I think you need to do something funny using items here, so look around!" I urged. Xander nodded in agreement and ran around the room looking for things to use.

"This doll is so annoying! It is so loud that I can't think!" he shouted.

"I think that was the point. It's there to distract you," Ashley said.

Xander paused for a moment as he stood in front of a closed box. He frantically opened it and uncovered three red balls. Without saying anything, he began juggling them.

"Huh. I didn't know you could juggle," I said. Xander didn't acknowledge me. He was too focused on the task at hand. As he juggled, he also performed a cartwheel, followed by a backflip. He didn't even drop one ball.

The horrible sound came to a halt and a square hole appeared, followed by another elevator.

"You did it, but how? That was amazing, Xander!" I cheered.

“Wait, guys, we have no idea what’s next! Let’s stay focused here!” warned Ashley. She was right, we didn’t know who or what we were up against, but hopefully we could work as a team and beat this.

Just as we were about to enter the elevator, we noticed a sign on the doors.

Maximum capacity = 8

“Oh no, one of us can’t fit...” I said.

“What should we do? There must be a way,” replied Bradley, whose costume was really confusing.

“Wait, what are you supposed to be?” I asked. Bradley was dressed in a long black gown with his face painted white.

"I am the bogeyman..." Bradley said, like it was obvious. I smiled and nodded, hoping I looked like I got it.

"I'll stay. I'm pretty exhausted after that challenge anyway," Xander said. Was he really going to stay *here*?

"Oh no, come with us!" I pleaded. Xander shook his head in protest.

"I'm no good to you guys like this. I'll find a spot here to nap. Don't worry, just go!" We all looked at each other before hesitantly walking back into the elevator—and back into the unknown.

4

To Make a Monster

When we entered the elevator this time, it moved right then left then right. It was as though we were in a maze. None of us said anything during the short journey, mostly because we were so worried about what was in store for us next.

Eventually, the elevator came to a stop and the doors opened. We stepped out one by one to assess the new room and the situation at hand. The room was fairly bare, with steel walls and a steel floor, something you might expect in a surgery room. One thing that immediately caught my attention was a steel table in the middle of the room, with a random assortment of boxes on top.

"That looks like a table for surgery..." whispered Bradley.

Welcome to room two. To escape this room, you must use every part of the body—but not any of your own parts. Time is ticking...

It was the strange voice again. What could it possibly mean?

We each took a box, opened it, and peeked inside.

"Gross, an arm!"

"Even more gross, a head!"

"I got a leg here!"

"Wait, the boxes are full of body parts? What are we supposed to do with them?" I blurted out. Everyone shrugged in confusion. Moments after we had opened the boxes, the room started to become warmer. Robin, who was dressed as Frankenstein, walked around the table carefully, trying to find further clues. He paused for a moment after his short investigation.

"The table is mostly made of steel, but its rim is all wood. Weird. I mean, it's painted to look like the steel..." he mused.

"It's getting hot in here, guys!" Ashley said in alarm.

"It would seem we have triggered something by opening the boxes. And since this room is metal, we are going to get completely roasted!" Robin cried.

Great. Getting charbroiled was definitely *not* on my bucket list.

We still had no idea about the challenge or how to escape. Robin dashed around the room, poking his face inside each box to get a better understanding.

"Guys," he said, "these body parts are some kind of plastic. They're already starting to melt. We have to hurry!"

"OK," Ashley said, "well, I think it's pretty obvious we need to put them together to make something. Like a monster, I guess."

"Well, this stuff is already hot," said Robin. "I need gloves. Quick, everyone, look around!" We all explored the steel room as fast as possible trying to find gloves for Robin, but it was so empty that we couldn't find anything.

"Maybe you don't need gloves if you don't touch the plastic?" suggested Ashley. What was she talking about? He needed to touch the plastic, right?

Robin smacked his head. "Of course! I'll tear off pieces of the boxes and use them to push the parts around. Everyone, start dumping the parts onto the table!"

It was getting so hot inside that I could feel my costume sticking to me.

After about thirty seconds, Robin stepped back and looked at his creation. It wasn't going to be mistaken for a real body any time soon, but I hoped it would do the trick. Even if it was a little mushy at this point.

"Did I do it? Did I do the challenge?" wondered Robin.

"It's getting cooler, that's for sure!" Ashley said. She was right; the temperature was dropping, and we all collectively let out a sigh of relief. Before we could even decide what to do next, a hole opened above us and the elevator slowly descended to take us to the next escape room.

“Well done, Robin!” I said happily. But something was telling me that we were far from finished. The last time we got into the elevator, somebody had to stay behind, and it was likely this was going to be the case again.

As the elevator doors opened, we noticed that the interior was smaller than before. We all tried to fit inside, but no amount of squeezing did the trick.

“I think you should stay, Pearl. You have hardly said anything or done anything to help us!” said Gwen.

“Well, I think *you* should stay, Gwen. You haven’t done anything either!” said Naomi.

“Stop this! Listen!” I shouted. “Time is not on our side here. We can try to figure out who will stay, but it will only just waste precious time. Robin, do you mind staying? I think that's what makes the most sense—the person who just did their part stays behind."

Everyone reluctantly nodded.

"Sure thing. I'll be ok, I promise!" said Robin. We each gave him a hug and headed into the elevator for the next challenge.

5

This Room Sucks!

The elevator came to a standstill after a few excruciating minutes. I could tell that none of us wanted to leave, as it meant facing the next challenge. Unfortunately, we had no choice, and we had to go into the unknown once more.

The elevator door opened to a room that was dimly lit, decorated in red velvet and black silk. There were three large coffee tables in the middle of the room, each covered in a red blanket.

"Whoa, kind of fancy," I noted.

"Search for something that looks out of place, guys!" said Ashley. That was tough. It seemed like a pretty normal kind of room—as normal as any of this was, of course—but maybe that was part of the challenge.

Pearl pointed at something that drew everyone's attention in a heartbeat. "Are those mirrors? Why can't we see our reflection in them?"

Pearl *was* pointing at a collection of mirrors on a wall, and she was right; there was no reflection in any of them, and that wasn't the only odd thing.

"Hey, Pearl, where is your makeup?" I asked. Pearl laughed for a second until she realized I was being serious.

"It took me hours to do my makeup. You can't possibly think I don't have any on!" she said. Everyone went silent. Pearl was a master of makeup, but when she did her videos, it always seemed as though it took under a minute to complete a makeover. We never knew it could take her hours to do it.

"Stacey is right, your makeup is totally gone!" confirmed Ashley.

Hello, TikTokers, and welcome to room three. This room might seem pretty nice, but I would advise you to be as quiet as mice. Think of this room as a great opportunity to fit in...

We all shrugged at each other. What was with these dumb riddles?

"Quiet as mice? What does that even mean?" Bradley muttered.

"Shhh! I think it means we might end up waking up something in here!" Ashley said.

"There's no one here, though," I whispered. Ashley placed her finger to her lips and pointed to the coffee tables in the middle of the room. Everyone shrugged in confusion yet again. Ashley rolled her eyes in frustration before heading over to the coffee tables and pulling off the red blankets that covered them.

"Coffins!" I shouted. Ashley shot me a dirty look and mouthed, *shh!*

“Worse, vampires!” she whispered.

“What do we do?” I said. Ashley navigated around the coffins, studying each closely. She paused to think.

“I think we should open it!” she whispered. Open a *coffin*? Yeah, *great* idea. Sheesh. There could be a vampire in there.

Nobody was nominating themselves to open the coffin, so Ashley took a deep breath and reached for the lid.

As it creaked open, we saw... an assortment of makeup inside.

“OK,” I said. “I did not see that coming.”

Ashley pointed to Pearl and then to the makeup. Pearl stepped forward and smiled.

“That voice said to try to fit in. I’m dressed as a vampire, but I don’t look like a vampire. I need to do my makeup again!” she said.

“But how can you do makeup when you can’t see yourself in the mirror?” I asked.

“That’s the whole challenge! She has to put on makeup without using a mirror,” Ashley blurted.

Pearl took a deep breath and pulled out a makeup box. She studied it closely before rubbing her face with a huge brush, turning her completely white. Then she pulled out eyeliner, lipstick and many other items. From where I stood, it appeared as though she was going crazy as she quickly threw everything on. Pearl lifted her face and we all screamed—she looked exactly like a vampire.

"Finished!" she said proudly, then looked around expectantly.

"Opportunity to fit in…" Ashley said with a grimace. "Pearl, I think you have to get inside the coffin."

Pearl shook her head in protest.

"I-I can't!" she stuttered. "No. I completed the challenge!"

"There's no time to argue here! Get your butt in that coffin!" Ashley demanded. She was so level-headed here, and she seemed to know a lot about escape rooms, which made me a little suspicious.

Pearl nodded and hesitantly lifted herself up and into the coffin, trembling.

A hole in the roof opened above us and the elevator descended once again. As the elevator thudded onto the ground, the coffin that Pearl was still inside moved.

"Get out, quick!" I shrieked. Pearl tried to climb out of the coffin, but it began to sink into the floor.

"Pearl!!" I shouted.

"There's no time; we need to get into the elevator now, please. Trust me, Stacey!" cried Ashley. She was right. There was little we could do, and time was running out. We all darted into the elevator, knowing that the chances of losing another of our group was highly likely.

6
Water World

During the very short journey in the elevator, I took the chance to ask Ashley how she knew so much about this stuff. I mean, she was like a detective.

"So, Ashley, how do you know so much about escape rooms?" I asked casually.

"Yeah, you sure know how to solve a problem very quickly!" added Bradley. Ashley bit her lip as she thought. Before she provided an answer, the elevator came to a halt, and cold water began seeping in.

"We have no time to talk about this, please!" said Ashley. How convenient... But I had to let it go for now.

The elevator doors opened to reveal a room filled with water, with what looked like a beach on the other side. There was a thick fog that lingered, preventing us from seeing anything farther.

"So, what is this room about?" I wondered. I stared directly at Ashley for an answer, but she looked away.

"Let's just do this!" Bradley snapped. As we each took a step into this room, we stumbled into what seemed like a shallow pool.

"Let's make it to the beach over there, and we can figure out the rest once we reach it," Ashley said, taking charge again. We all slowly drifted through the water toward the beach.

"All right, we know the drill by now! Look for clues," I said. We split up to explore this small beach to figure out what this challenge could be about.

"Hey, I found something!" yelled Gwen. We all scurried over to investigate.

Gwen was standing near a collection of seashells in a strange formation.

"It's just seashells, Gwen!" I moaned. Ashley shook her head.

"No, it's trying to form a sentence. Just don't touch anything," Ashley said. It was too late. Gwen was holding one of the shells in her hand.

Hello again, TikTokers. I hope you are enjoying the beach, but not for long. Looks like the tide is coming in. If you 'gather' your ideas, you might just get out alive.

Oh great, our new friend again.

We all stood there in silence until Ashley stepped forward.

"So, you picked up one of those seashells, which has triggered the challenge, and the tide is going to come in and take us all. The shells form a word, I think," replied Ashley.

"OK, so where are the rest?" added Bradley. "There aren't enough here for any words I can think of." Ashley glared into the water pointedly.

"Wait, somebody needs to go into the water and retrieve the rest? Who can do that?" I asked. "There's a reason I never joined the swim team, just saying."

Gwen took a step forward and let out a big sigh.

"I've been scuba diving and swimming ever since I can remember. I can do this. And anyway, I'm dressed as a mermaid!" she said. Gwen was the most athletic of us all, so I believed she could easily do this challenge. The tide was coming in faster than we realized, with each of us having to take a step back already.

"Please, Gwen, go for it!" Ashley urged. Gwen nodded and jumped into the water without any fear. I was impressed. As we looked into the water, we saw bubbles float to the surface, but Gwen was nowhere to be seen.

"Hey, where is she?" I called. "It must be deeper than I thought." But Gwen surfaced then, throwing a few shells onto the shore. She dived down again and popped up once more. The seashells were of different colors and shapes to the ones on the beach. Gwen surfaced once more, swimming back to the tiny beach we were all stuck on.

"Guys, when I was underwater, I could hear the seashells. They told me the word!" Gwen said, catching her breath.

"I know what to do! It sounds weird but I heard a voice under the water!" Gwen continued. I really hoped she wasn't losing it. We did not have time for that.

Gwen majestically stepped in front of the shells already on the beach, ignoring us all.

Soon she revealed the word **ESCAPE**.

As soon as Gwen moved the seashells, the small body of water surrounding us began to recede.

"It worked!" yelled Ashley, just as the last of the water drained away to reveal another elevator hatch.

"Guys, I can't move!" shrieked Gwen. The sand that she was standing on had turned into quicksand. She was sinking!

"Quit fooling around, Gwen, we don't need this!" I shouted. Gwen shook her head. "I'm not joking! I really can't move!"

"I'm sorry—we need to go. Please forgive us!" Ashley said. We all looked in horror at Gwen, who was struggling to keep herself from sinking.

You have five seconds. Four. Three... the now-familiar voice said from somewhere out of view.

We didn't have time to argue or help. We knew if we didn't get into that elevator then we too would be stuck in this room. Everyone ran into the elevator just before the doors shut tight, leaving behind our beloved friend Gwen in the process.

7

Oh, Mummy!

The elevator felt different this time around, as though it was rotating. When it did finally come to a halt, I felt a little green around the gills. The doors opened and we each took a slow step forward, uncovering what appeared to be a tomb. The floor was made of sand, the walls were covered in strange graffiti, and there were sarcophagi lining each wall.

"OK, everyone, keep your hands to yourself and look around!" Ashley ordered. As we each set off to explore the new room, we heard a strange *click*.

"You didn't say anything about feet!" moaned Naomi, who had stepped on a tile, likely triggering something.

Welcome, TikTokers. As a kid, your mummy probably sang you to sleep. I would advise you to do the opposite now.

We all glared at Naomi, who seemed afraid to move. The sarcophagi in the room were shaking erratically, as though something was going to pop out of them.

"Uh, we need to figure out the challenge *now* before those weird coffins burst open!" I whispered. "What about the graffiti? It must mean something!"

"That's not graffiti. It's hieroglyphics. I mean, this tomb appears Egyptian, and I'm going to take a wild guess here and say that there are probably mummies in those coffins," Ashley said.

Naomi chuckled for a moment before taking a deep breath.

"It's not graffiti, and it's certainly not hieroglyphics. It's musical notes, you know, for singing?" suggested Naomi. She was the only member of our group who could sing; in fact, she was really good at it. I couldn't help but speculate that maybe this challenge was for her.

"That voice said something about how our moms would sing us to sleep and to do the opposite... Oh! I got it.

You need to sing to put the *mummies* to sleep!" Bradley said, figuring out the challenge before Ashley for a change.

"But I have no idea where to start. I mean, it's all over the place!" Naomi said nervously.

"Wait, what about that tile you stepped on? Take a closer look at it!" encouraged Ashley. Naomi removed her foot from the tile and noticed an arrow.

"It's pointing to this side of the wall. It has to be it!" shouted Naomi. It was getting harder and harder to hear each other as the sarcophagus lids shook faster and louder.

"Do it! Sing! I mean, you are dressed as a mummy for Halloween—this challenge is for you!" I yelled. Naomi nodded and took a deep breath before singing the notes on the walls. She must have sung every note there ever was; it was incredible. From low notes to high notes to *really* high notes.

Suddenly there was silence, and one of the sarcophagi moved to the side, revealing the elevator.

“You did it! Well done!” I clapped in relief. Naomi beamed as she walked towards the elevator to join the rest of us inside. Just as she reached the threshold, one of the spooky sarcophagui flung open and a mummy jumped out and grabbed Naomi, pulling her in.

“Nooooo!” I wailed.

But before I could leave the elevator, its doors shut tight. I exploded into tears. Were we really going to be picked off until no one was left?

8

Boogie, Man

The elevator doors opened to a room that we all could recognize easily as a bedroom. It looked totally normal with a bed, a bookcase, even a computer on a small desk.

"T-T-This is my bedroom!" stuttered Bradley. His bedroom? Huh. I would have thought it'd be messier.

"Let's just get this over with. Find something to trigger the challenge, y'all,"

Ashley said. I was starting to get a little tired of the bossiness, if I'm being honest.

"No, please don't touch my stuff!" Bradley said, blushing. Ashley stared at him for a second before rolling her eyes.

"Fine, we can just stay in your bedroom forever. I hope you don't mind sharing your bed with me, Stacey, and Diego! By the way, did you always have this giant elevator in the middle of the room?" she said sarcastically. Bradley huffed and then slumped in defeat.

Bradley's bedroom was pretty small, so it wasn't too hard to explore, but we couldn't find anything.

"I know my room better than all of you," sighed Bradley as he fell to his knees and crawled under his bed, pulling out a small radio.

"Maybe we can use this to try and get some help?" he said.

He switched on the radio and suddenly the entire room went pitch black.

Welcome, TikTokers. This room might look pretty safe—if you could see, that is. Sometimes, a bump in the night is a good thing...

I could feel heavy breath behind me. I knew there was something present in the room aside from my friends, but I didn't want to say anything and make everyone panic.

"OK, smarty pants, since this is your room, then maybe you know what to do next?" Ashley said.

"Wait, you don't know this one? That's novel," I replied.

"What is that supposed to mean? And why did you just touch my leg?" Ashley snapped.

"I didn't touch your leg. It must have been Diego!" I hissed. *Or the thing that's in here with us...*

"It wasn't me!" said Diego. "But who is touching my arm?"

"Stop it, guys. It's obvious we are not alone in this room. We need a light," shouted Bradley. As he attempted to move around the room in complete darkness, he missed a step and stumbled, twisting, which resulted in him glowing for a split second.

"What was that, Bradley? And who is touching my feet? Stop it!" I yelled.

"Bradley, try to do another spin there!" Ashley called. Bradley placed his feet together before doing a spin, illuminating himself again for a second.

"Hey, the hands left my feet after you did that..." I said.

"Same, do it again!" begged Ashley. Bradley did another spin, this one a little longer than before, resulting in a longer bright light emitting from him.

"Oh, I figured it out. You are dressed as the bogeyman, so you have to *boogie*. Each time you dance, it keeps the monsters in this room away from us because the because the bogeyman hates light," Ashley said. "I guess we've moved on to the dad joke portion of the evening."

Bradley burst into a vivid display of dance moves. He performed spins, flips, and handstands, illuminating the room with each move.

"It's working, nothing is touching me!" I rejoiced. As Bradley continued to dance, the bedroom slowly lit up.

"Keep going!" I cheered. When the lights were fully on, the elevator appeared again.

"Well done, Bradley, now let's get out of here!" I shouted. As we all darted back into the elevator, the large closet in the room opened dramatically.

"Get in quickly, Bradley!" I called. He tried to race into the elevator, but a long web shot out of the closet, wrapped around Bradley's legs, and dragged him in.

"No! We need to save him, please!" I yelled. "Not another one!"

"We can't, Stacey, we just don't have the time!" hissed Ashley as she grabbed me by the arm, preventing me from running out. The elevator doors shut as I watch Bradley get pulled into the closet.

9

Toil and Trouble

I still couldn't believe that we had lost so many of us. During the short journey in the elevator, I took a moment to reflect on the situation. Who was next to do a challenge? What if we couldn't figure one out? Who were we going to lose next? So many questions clouded my mind that I didn't even notice that the elevator had come to a halt.

"Stacey? Let's go! Now!" Ashley called, snapping her fingers in my face.

I was trying my best not to cry and be as strong as possible, but it was so difficult. As I stepped into the new room, I noticed how much it looked like a kitchen—a very gross, dirty, disgusting one. There was an open fire on one side, and a huge cauldron in the middle of the room. I also saw a table with lots of random spices and herbs. The entire ceiling was covered in cobwebs, and I lost count of how many spiders I saw.

"Well, I just lost my appetite!" joked Ashley.

We all explored the dirty kitchen, trying to figure out what this challenge was all about. I peeked inside the huge cauldron to find it empty; maybe something needed to go inside?

"This is driving me crazy, guys; you know I love to cook. I just want to clean this place!" groaned Diego. He grabbed a broom that was hanging on one of the walls. Suddenly, we heard loud meows coming from every corner. Cats began pouring into the room, from the cupboards, from the holes in the floorboards, from *everywhere*. We were surrounded by cats, and these were definitely *not* the petting kind.

"Cats are my phobie!" Diego shrieked. Huh. All right.

"These kitties look like they want to bite us! Bad kitties!" yelled Ashley.

Welcome, TikTokers. Looks like the cats are out of the bag. Better figure out how to get them back in... unless you want to stay here with them...

“Has anyone here ever owned a cat?” asked Ashley. We all shrugged.

“OK, so does anyone here *know* anything about cats?” she tried. We all shrugged.

“Great, then we’re all done for! Soon, these kitties are going to attack us, and then that’s it!”

“We’re in a kitchen. I’m sure there are many things in here that we can use to help us!” said Diego.

“You mean like... create a cat repellent?” Ashley ventured. Diego nodded with a smile.

"None of us know anything about cooking except you, Diego. And you're dressed as a cat. Wait, why are you dressed as your phobia?" I said.

"I'm supposed to be a witch, actually. I can't believe you think I look like a *cat*," he said with a shudder. "Anyway, I need to explore this kitchen, but they're all in the way. You guys are going to have to distract them!" Great. I didn't know much about cats, but I had heard how hard it's supposed to be to herd kittens...

"What are we going to do? They're hissing like crazy!" Ashley cried.

"There's no time, do it now!" Diego shouted. Just then, I noticed a piece of string hanging off Ashley's ghost costume.

"I have an idea! Just trust me!" I said. I grabbed onto the string and pulled at it until it came loose, quickly rolled it into a ball, and threw it into the crowd of cats. The felines scattered as I hurled the ball across the room, but then they all gave chase, rushing to investigate their new toy.

Diego used this distraction time effectively, running around the kitchen to find anything he could use. He knocked on cupboards before opening them in case a cat was inside. Poor guy.

He bent down and peeked under tables and chairs and finally returned to the counter with the cauldron, his arms full of supplies.

"I found garlic, chili, orange, rosemary, lemon…" Diego said, panting.

"Great, but you need to make a repellent, right? So, you need some kind of liquid to cook them all in," suggested Ashley. Diego's smile faded.

"I did see a mop with dirty water in it. I guess that will have to do," he said with a grimace. The idea of all those things mixed with dirty water made me want to be sick. Again. Why did this whole mess have to be so *gross*?

"The whole room will reek, but I guess we don't have a choice…" Ashley conceded. Diego rushed over to the mop bucket, lifting it over his head and pouring it into the cauldron. As the water boiled, he threw in his assortment of ingredients. The smell was borderline unbearable for us, but it was also pungent enough to make the crazy cats flee to their hiding spots.

The elevator door opened once more, revealing that the challenge must have been a success. Ashley and I knew the drill by this point and rushed in. Diego was close behind us but stumbled, crashing to the floor.

"Diego!" I shouted. "What's happening?"

"It's the repellent—it's so strong that it made him pass out!" Ashley explained. "He was the one who got the biggest whiff." Before I could go out and grab him, the elevator doors shut tight. Another friend lost, and only Ashley and me left to finish this nightmare...

10

Boo!

I wasn't sure I had the strength to continue through this whole ordeal. The elevator came to halt once more, but this time I refused to leave.

"I am not getting out of this elevator, Ashley! I want to know how you are so good with figuring out all of these challenges. I know you're hiding something here," I accused. Ashley was already outside of the elevator by this point.

"Please, we don't have time for this! We need to keep going!" she begged. I shook my head and crossed my arms stubbornly.

"Fine. This whole game... I... I created it," she admitted.

"What? This is all because of you? All of our friends lost because of *you*?"

"No, please, listen!" she cried, stepping toward me, but I shoved her away.

"Please, Stacey, don't do this! Let me explain!" I was so furious I had no idea what to do. The elevator door was slowly closing.

"Please!" she repeated. "I have no idea where this elevator could take you if you don't get out. Just come with me, and we'll figure this all out." She was sobbing now. As much as I wanted to stay in the elevator and avoid her completely, I knew I couldn't risk it. I rushed out of the elevator and into the new room.

"Thank you! I know you don't trust me right now, but I'm the only one left. I will explain everything once we get out of this, I promise!" she said. I ignored her and threw myself into figuring out the challenge.

This new room was completely empty except for what looked like mannequins with white sheets over them. It seemed each challenge was getting harder, and with very little around, it was going to be tough to crack.

Ashley probably knew the challenge, but I didn't want to talk to her or help her.

"There are only these strange ghosts..." I muttered to myself. I watched Ashley closely as she navigated the room, but it seemed as though she was having no luck either.

"You're going to have to talk to me at some point," she snapped.

"I don't have to do anything, actually!" I shot back. As I walked around the room, I realized that I had not even looked under the white sheets. I stood in front of one mannequin and pulled the white sheet off it, revealing only a plastic figure. I went up to the next one and the one after, doing the same thing over and over. Nothing.

Hello, TikTokers. It's amazing you have made it this far. You are probably as white as a sheet right now... Just make sure it doesn't stay that way...

"What does that mean?" I said. I looked at Ashley, but she appeared as confused as me. In fact, she was really pale, and not because she was already dressed as a ghost.

"You are, like, *really* white," I told her, forgetting my vow not to speak to her. Ashley placed her hands in front of her face and screamed. "I'm turning into a ghost!" This didn't make any sense; I didn't think I had triggered the challenge.

"Why did you do this? *Why*?" I shouted. Ashley cried as I demanded an answer.

"Please, help me with this! I need your help!" she begged. I really didn't want to, but I needed answers. I rushed around the room once more, this time inspecting the strange mannequins. As I reached out to touch one, I realized that I too was turning pale.

I screamed, then turned back to Ashley.

"Ok, I think I have it figured out. Each time we move, we turn more and more pale. We need to stand still like these mannequins. Freeze," said Ashley. I was running around the room at this point, freaking out.

"I can't, this is terrifying!" I shouted.

"Please, just trust me!" she said. I *didn't* trust her, but I did as she said. We both stood frozen, resulting in our skin color slowly turning back to normal.

"Listen, I wrote a short story about escape rooms last year for a competition. This *was* the story. Someone took the story and turned it into a reality. I mean, most of it is pretty much the same, but some things were changed," she explained.

"That's... totally insane," I uttered carefully, trying my best not to move my face much.

I could barely see Ashley, but I caught a glimpse of a single tear falling from her face to the ground.

Suddenly, the elevator door burst open, and Ashley and I could finally move.

“We did it!” I cheered. I ran over to give Ashley a hug but... I couldn’t feel her.

I gasped, and Ashley burst into tears on the discovery. She was a ghost!

“Listen, the last challenge is on you,” she said. “You only have a few seconds to get into that elevator! If this is all based on my story, then remember that to escape the final room and this entire thing, you need to use the elevator and...”

But before she could finish, she was gone.

11

Back from the Dead

I was all alone and dreading the next room and the next challenge. I had lost a friend each time we were in one of the rooms, and who knew what happened to them when they got stuck there? I just hoped that if I beat the challenge, I could actually escape. It seemed more like it was not an escape room at all but just one big trap.

Then it dawned on me. What if I found a way to escape *before* completing the challenge?

The elevator doors opened and fog stormed inside. Just before I took a step forward, I remembered what Ashley had said to me. She had told me to use the elevator—if only she'd had time to finish her sentence!

I knew as soon as I left the elevator the doors would shut, but maybe, just maybe, I could stop that somehow...

I checked my costume to see if I had anything useful. I felt my phone, which had no signal and was about to die anyway. I had only recently gotten this phone, and I really didn't want to break it, but then again, I would much rather have a broken phone than be stuck inside this place.

I aligned my phone on the ground where the elevator doors would shut, thinking my phone might stop the doors shutting completely. It was crazy, but it might just work. What did I have to lose, anyway?

Well, except my phone.

As I stepped out of the elevator, I watched the doors begin to close, but my trusty phone did its job. Thank you, technology!

I turned around slowly to investigate the room I was in. It was very dark, but I could make out an array of graves. Great. A cemetery. And I was alone. I had never been so scared in my life, but I needed to find a way out. As I paced around the room trembling in fear, I noticed each grave had the name of someone from my friend group.

So they were dead. I really was alone. I wanted to sink to my knees and cry, but I had to focus if I wanted to get out of here alive. I saw a bunch of wild daisies in the center of the room, the only pretty thing there. I walked over and pulled a few from the ground, placing one flower each at my friends' graves. Suddenly, there was a flash of lightning and the graves vibrated.

Welcome, Stacey. Looks like you are the last one. A reunion of sorts is underway, though you might struggle to know your friends from your foes...

I must have triggered the challenge with the flowers. To make matters worse, I could see the dirt over the graves moving up and down. I was dressed as a zombie, so this could only mean that I was going to deal with zombies. But not just any zombies—my friends. I ran around the graveyard looking for something to help me. Just as I was about to give up, I saw a bright light from the sky.

“Stacey, it’s me. Well, ghost me!”

“Ashley! How are—”

“I can, like, walk through walls and stuff. This challenge involves these zombies coming out of their graves, and you have to beat them back in. A bit like whack-a-mole, really. But listen. You *cannot* finish the challenge!" she said.

"Then what should I do? Please, tell me!"

"You need to escape through the elevator. There is a secret door at the top. Go through it and climb your way to the top until you reach a door. That is the control room for everything," she said. "I need to go. Good luck!"

"Please don't go!" I begged. As Ashley floated up to the sky, I could see hands erupt from the graves and then zombie versions of my friends emerge. I was so terrified that I couldn't even move. As they all crawled out of the ground, the zombies surrounded me. I had nowhere to hide.

12
The Final Scare

As the zombies approached me, I kept stepping backward until I felt a hard surface behind me. The zombies slowly crept closer until they had me cornered. This was truly the end. I closed my eyes and took a deep breath, anticipating my untimely demise.

During this moment, I placed my hands behind me, hoping to grab onto something, and that was when I felt cold and metallic. The elevator! Duh! I spun around as fast as I could, squeezed my fingers through the small space, and pulled the doors open with all of my strength. I managed to squeeze through. As soon as I got inside, the doors shut tight, and I heard the zombies banging outside. And then the voice came back.

Hey, get back out there!

I took a deep breath and wiped the tears from my eyes. Since I was temporarily shielded from these monsters, it gave me a short moment to think, and I remembered Ashley telling me that the elevator had a secret door at the top. I tilted my head up and spotted it.

I bent my knees and readied myself for a huge jump. I sprang from the floor with all my might and managed to burst through the secret door using my head. I grabbed the edges and pulled myself up and through the secret door, finding a long ladder. It was probably the longest ladder I had ever seen, but I wasn't ready to give up just yet. I needed to finish this, save my friends—who Ashley seemed to think weren't really dead—and maybe even enjoy the rest of my Halloween.

I took my first step onto the ladder, found it was sturdy enough to carry me, and slowly made my way to the top. I didn't think about looking down or falling off; all I could think about was finishing this once and for all.

At the top, I located a small door and heard loud mechanical sounds inside.

I pulled the door open with every once of strength I had and squeezed through, entering a room full of computers and bright lights.

Either I'd found the control room, or this was another escape room. There was an array of screens, which looked like CCTV, and as I stared, I saw that each one showed an escape room I had previously been in. This meant that there were cameras in all of those rooms, somebody had been watching us, and it must have been this figure in front of me.

I could confront the culprit, but then I realized something. This person had been scaring everyone, so why not give them a taste of their own medicine?

I took lumbering steps and made weird growling sounds. I wanted the mastermind behind all of this to think that I was an actual zombie.

He turned around.

"Benny! I should have known!" I yelled.

"Stacey? You aren't a zombie, are you?" asked Benny cautiously.

"I got bitten. I'm slowly turning into one, actually, and you look pretty delicious!" I figured I may as well stick with the plan.

"Wait, don't eat me!" he begged.

"Well, I dunno, all these challenges have made me very hungry!" I couldn't keep it up, though. "You *jerk.*"

He rolled his eyes. "OK, Stacey. I knew you weren't actually a zombie. Anyway, I needed you all to perform fresh TikToks for my account, and since you all did such a good job, I'm keeping you in the rooms to do more and more. I'm going to be filthy rich," Benny said. "I would have never come up with the idea if not for Ashley and her little story. She must learn to reset her password every once in a while! But I guess since you're here, I'm going to have to come up with something else. Thanks a lot..."

Benny turned around and pushed some buttons on the main computer, and suddenly everything in the room shook erratically. An elevator opened up and all of my friends came out.

"Quick, guys," I said. "Help me eat this bozo... I'm a zooooombie!"

"I want to turn him into a soup first!" Diego said.

"I want to wrap him up in bandages!" Naomi called.

"I think I will suck his blood!" Pearl added.

"I want to take him apart and only *maybe* put him back together!" Robin shouted.

"I think I will take his soul!" Ashley said.

"I plan on turning him into a balloon animal!" Xander said, cracking a smile.

"I'm going to pull him into the ocean!" Gwen declared.

"And I... I will show him why everyone is afraid of the bogeyman!" Bradley finished lamely.

Benny rushed past us all, heading toward the elevator to escape.

"Quick, someone stop him!" I shouted. Ashley sprinted into the elevator, pushing every button inside before jumping out. Benny screamed as the doors shut tight.

"What did you just do, Ashley?" I asked.

"I pushed every button in the elevator. This will completely break it. Basically, he has his very own escape room challenge now," she said. "And who knows when he will escape—or *if* he can escape!"

"So, now what do we do? How do we get out of here?" I asked. Ashley ran over to the main computer and pushed some buttons. A huge portal opened up in the middle of the room.

"Here we are! Everybody in!" she said. "I watched Benny make portals when I was a ghost."

"You were a *ghost*?" shrieked Pearl, who almost fainted in fear.

"OK, guys, no more scares, please!" I said.

Each one of my friends jumped through the portal until it was just me and Ashley. I was hesitating to do it as I still felt a little uneasy after everything that had happened between us.

“Can I really trust you?” I asked. I could see tears welling in her eyes.

“I don’t expect you to, but know that I will always consider you a friend,” she told me. We gave each other a hug and I jumped through the portal, which led me back to the entrance of the event hall.

* * *

As soon as I was home, I got out of my costume, made some popcorn, and put on a movie. My parents arrived pretty late, and they were both surprised to see me on the couch.

“You aren’t out celebrating Halloween with your friends? How was the award ceremony?” Mom asked.

“Oh, it turned out to be one big escape room adventure,” I said casually. “Come watch the movie!”

Mom went quiet and sat right next to me, giving me a big hug. As much as I enjoyed some quiet time, I still wondered one thing about the story, so I decided to send Ashley a message on my sad, cracked phone.

Hey Ashley, I was wondering, how did your story end?

Her reply came right away.

It ended with us becoming best friends…

Made in the USA
Monee, IL
04 October 2022

15220199R00062